PIANO • VOCAL

# BROADWAY SINGER'S edition

VOCAL WITH PIANO ACCOMPANIMENT

**Annie**

Pianist on the CD: Jamie Johns

ISBN 978-1-4768-9970-1

**HAL•LEONARD®**
CORPORATION
7777 W. BLUEMOUND RD. P.O. BOX 13819 MILWAUKEE, WI 53213

# Easy Street

Lyric by MARTIN CHARNIN
Music by CHARLES STROUSE

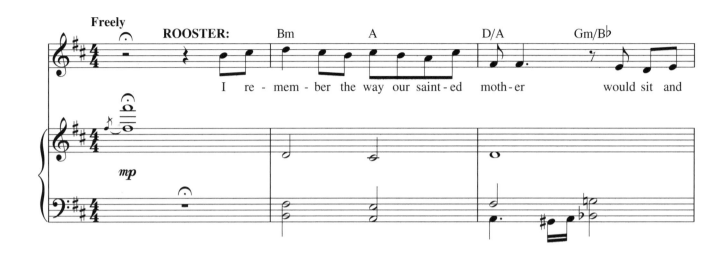

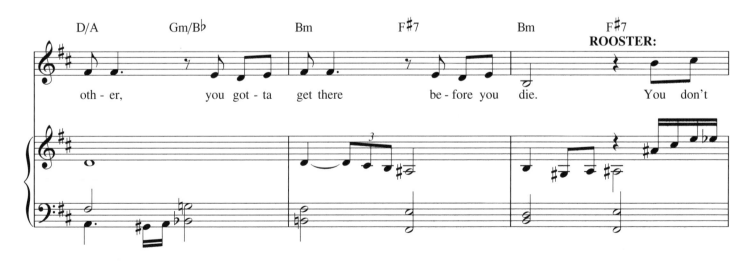

3

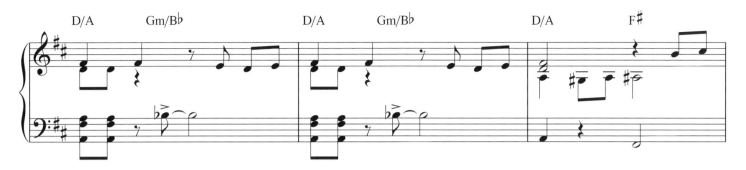

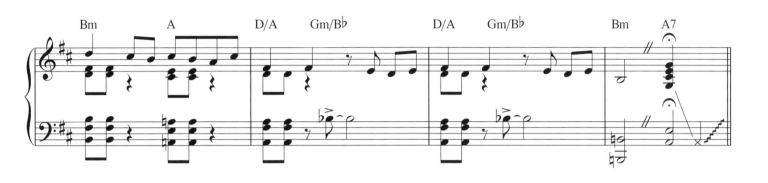

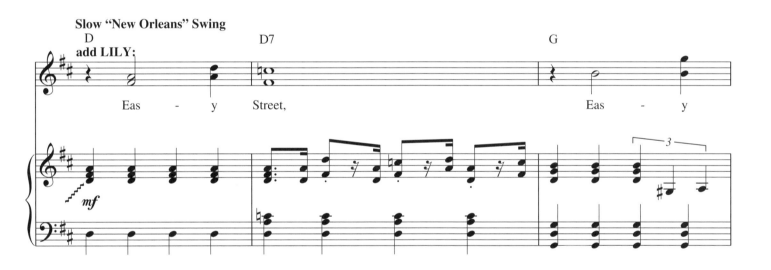

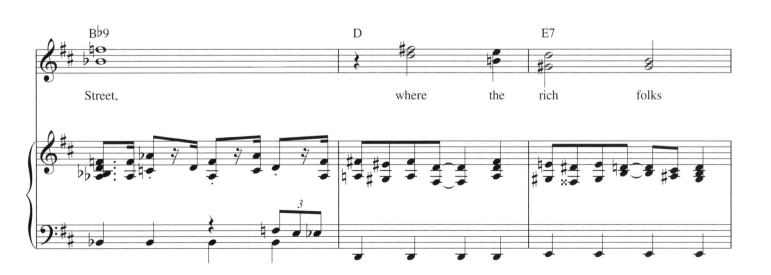

# I Don't Need Anything but You

Lyric by MARTIN CHARNIN
Music by CHARLES STROUSE

# Maybe

Lyric by MARTIN CHARNIN
Music by CHARLES STROUSE

they'll be there call - ing me "Ba - by," may -

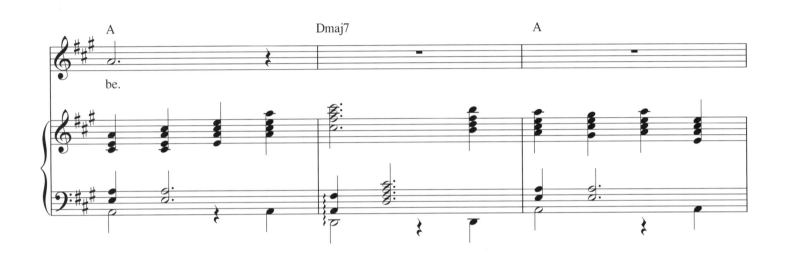

be.

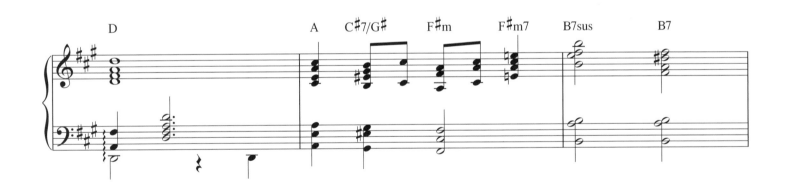

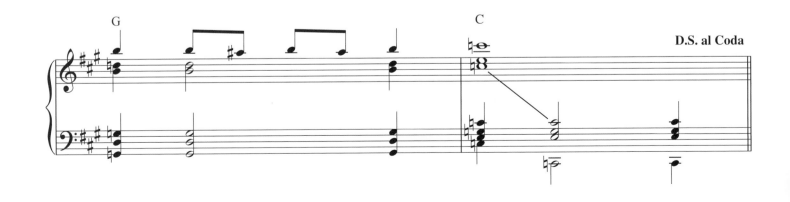

**D.S. al Coda**

# It's the Hard-Knock Life

Lyric by MARTIN CHARNIN
Music by CHARLES STROUSE

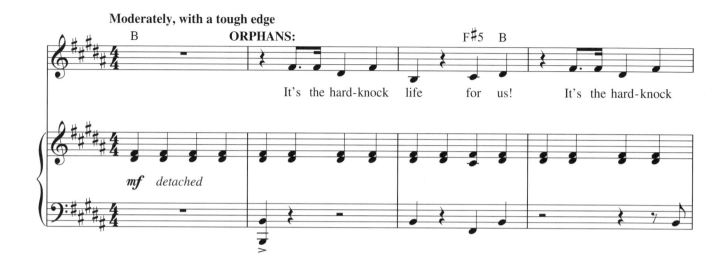

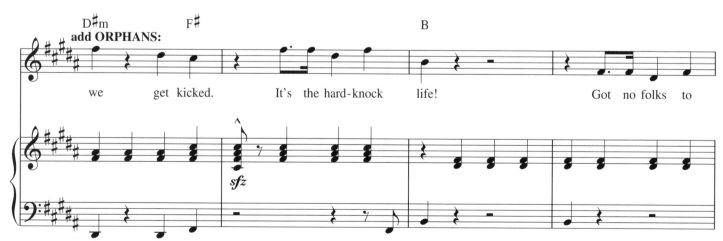

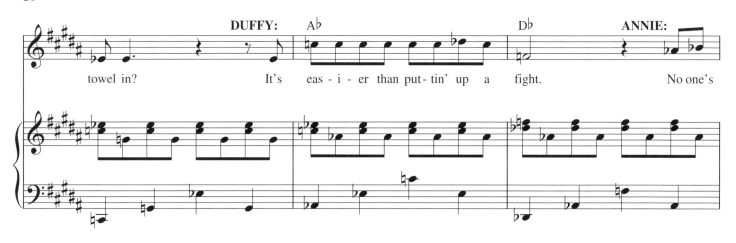

DUFFY: A♭ D♭ ANNIE:

towel in? It's eas-i-er than put-tin' up a fight. No one's

C♯m Bm

there when your dreams at night get creep-y. ___ No one cares if you grow or if you

ORPHANS:

Ooo ___ Ooo ___

Am ALL:

shrink. No one dries when your eyes get red and weep-y. ___ From the

___ Ooo ___

# Little Girls

Lyric by MARTIN CHARNIN
Music by CHARLES STROUSE

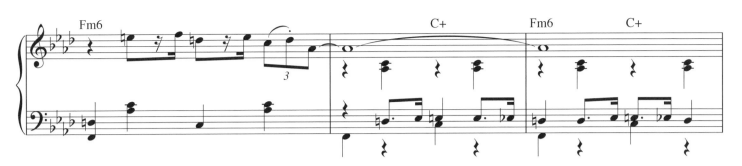

How I hate lit - tle shoes, lit - tle socks and each lit - tle bloom - er.___

I'd have cracked years a - go if it weren't for my sense of

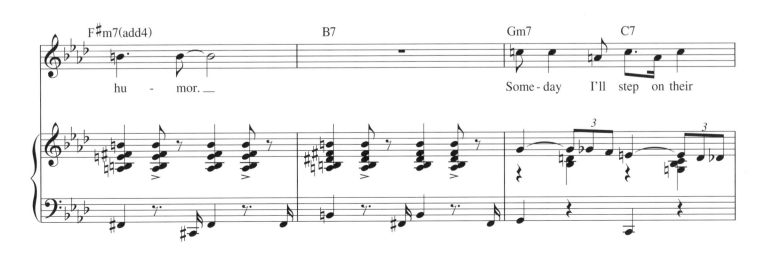

hu - mor.___ Some - day I'll step on their

# A New Deal for Christmas

Lyric by MARTIN CHARNIN
Music by CHARLES STROUSE

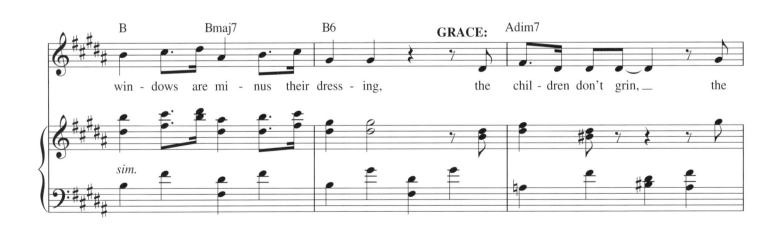

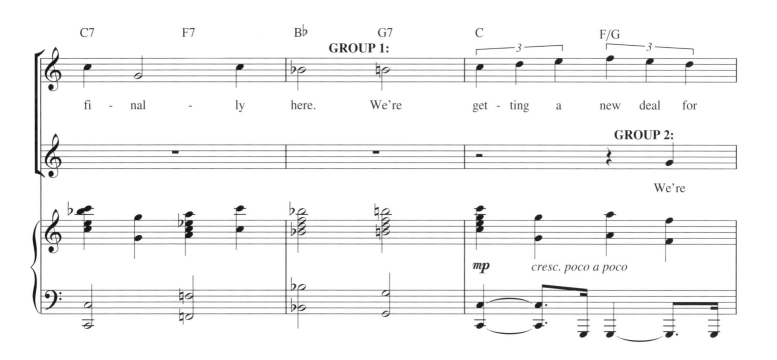

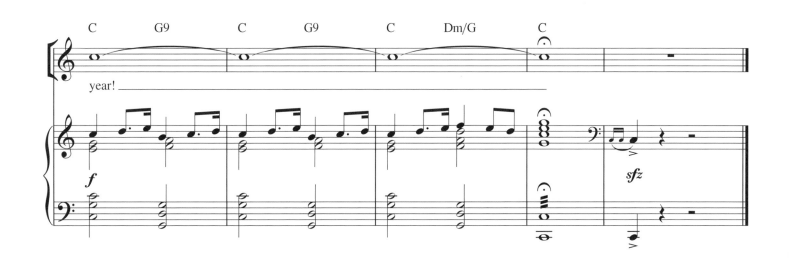

# Tomorrow

Lyric by MARTIN CHARNIN
Music by CHARLES STROUSE

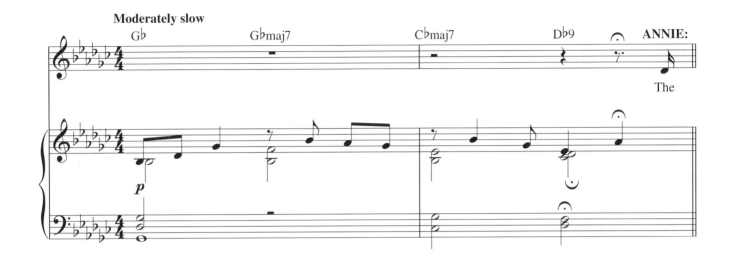

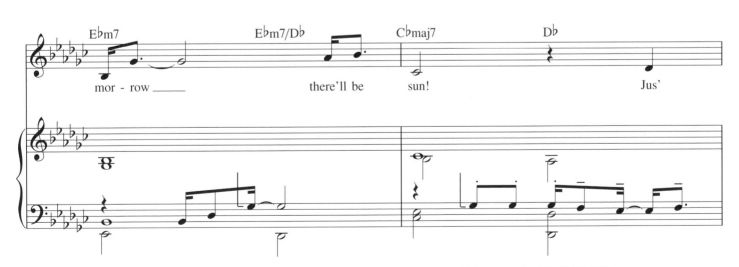

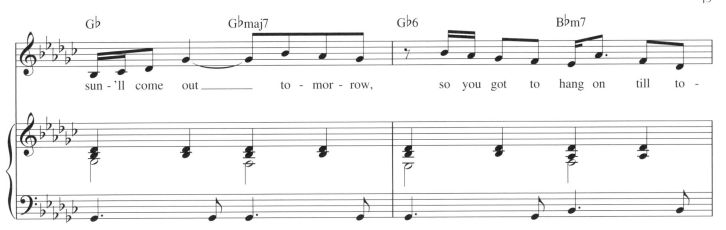

sun-'ll come out _____ to-mor-row, so you got to hang on till to-

mor-row ___ come what may! To - mor-row, to-mor-row, I

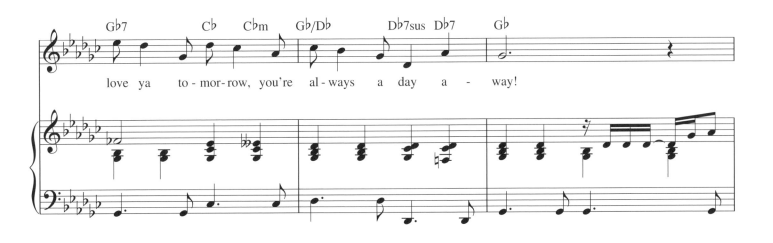

love ya to-mor-row, you're al-ways a day a - way!

# N.Y.C.

Lyric by MARTIN CHARNIN
Music by CHARLES STROUSE

a - gain        on N.        Y. C.

*f* [gradual accel.]

[Moderately fast]

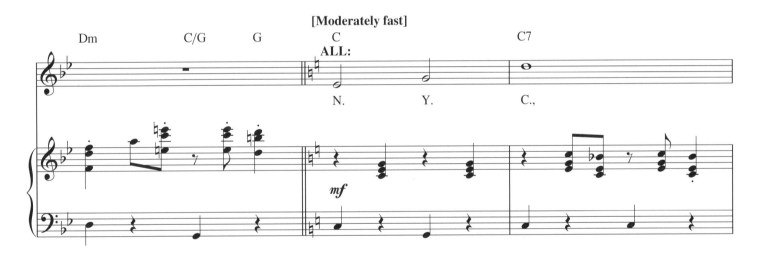

ALL:

N.       Y.       C.,

*mf*

[straight 8ths]

GRACE:

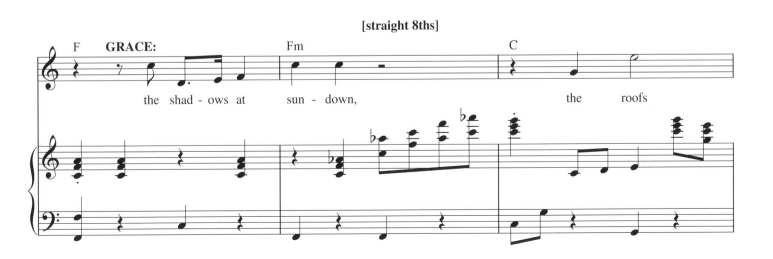

the shad - ows at     sun - down,         the roofs

you cramp, you're still the champ.

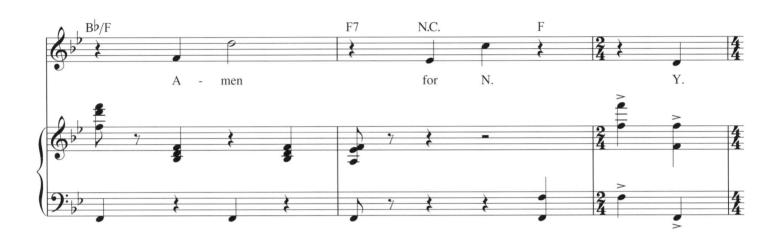

A - men for N. Y.

[Faster still, straight 8ths]

C.

# Something Was Missing

Lyric by MARTIN CHARNIN
Music by CHARLES STROUSE

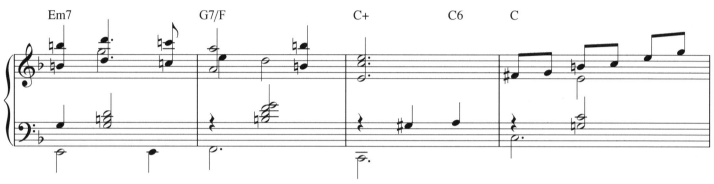

Who would need me for me, need me for

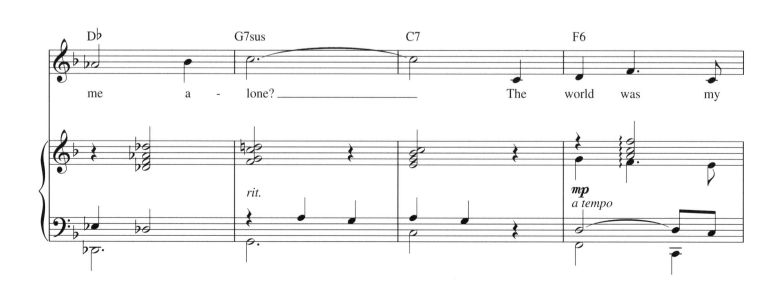

me a - lone? _____ The world was my

# You're Never Fully Dressed
# Without a Smile

Lyric by MARTIN CHARNIN
Music by CHARLES STROUSE

**Brightly, with a jaunty lilt**

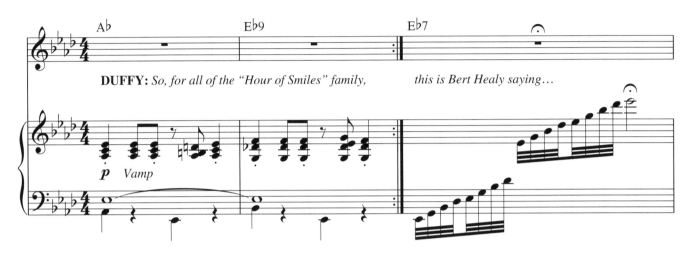

DUFFY: *So, for all of the "Hour of Smiles" family,* *this is Bert Healy saying…*

p Vamp

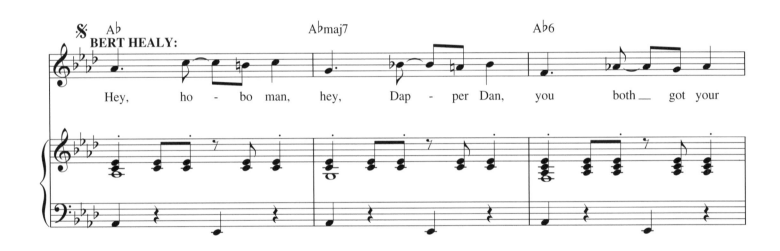

BERT HEALY:

Hey, ho - bo man, hey, Dap - per Dan, you both \_ got your

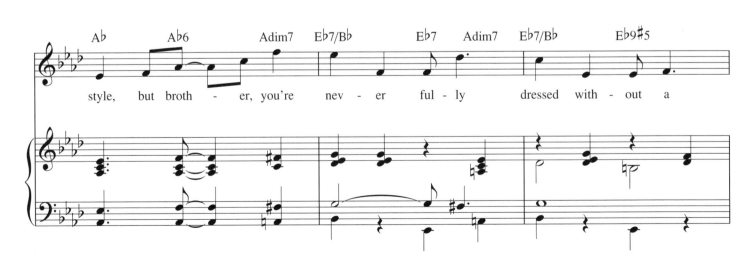

style, but broth - er, you're nev - er ful - ly dressed with - out a

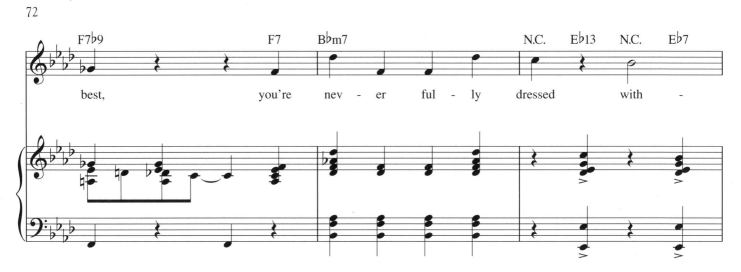

best, you're nev - er ful - ly dressed with -

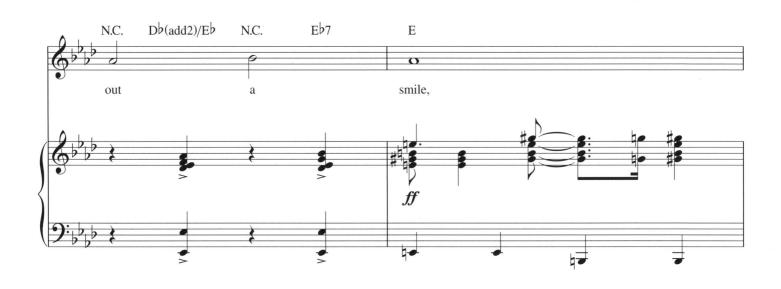

out a smile,

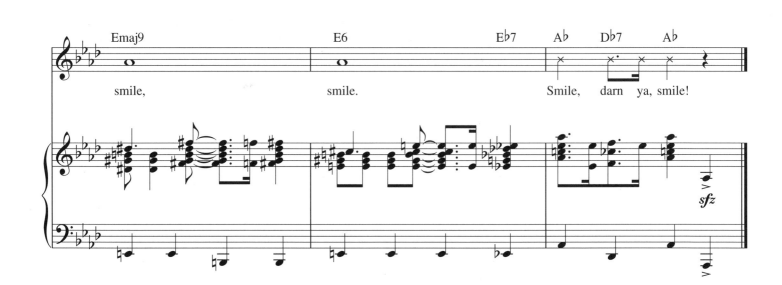

smile, smile. Smile, darn ya, smile!